GW00322645

barbecue

barbecue

Louise Pickford

photography by Ian Wallace

RYLAND
PETERS
& SMALL
LONDON NEW YORK

First published in Great Britain in 2004
by Ryland Peters & Small
Kirkman House
12–14 Whitfield Street
London WIT 2RP
www.rylandpeters.com

10 9 8 7 6 5 4 3 2 1

ISBN 1 84172 583 8

A CIP record for this book is available
from the British Library.

Designer Luana Gobbo
Commissioning Editor Elsa Petersen-Schepelern
Editor Sharon Ashman
Production Patricia Harrington
Art Director Gabriella Le Grazie
Publishing Director Alison Starling

Food and Props Stylist Louise Pickford
Indexer Hilary Bird

Acknowledgments

Beautiful props were provided by The
Baytree, Woollahra, NSW; Bison
Homewares, Queanbeyan, ACT
(www.bisonhome.com); Camargue,
Mosman, NSW; Tolle N Crowe,
Northbridge, NSW; Design Mode
International, Mona Vale, NSW; Village
Living, Avalon, NSW. Above all, a big
thank you to Weber Australia for their
help in supplying their huge range of
barbecues and equipment for the recipe
development and photography.
www.weberbbq.com.au

Notes

All spoon measurements are level unless
otherwise specified.

To sterilize preserving jars or bottles,
wash the jars in hot, soapy water and
rinse in boiling water. Put them in a large
saucepan and pour over enough water
to cover. With the lid on, bring the water
to the boil and continue boiling for
15 minutes. Turn off the heat, then leave
the jars in the hot water until just before
they are to be filled. Invert the jars onto
clean kitchen paper to dry. Sterilize the
lids for 5 minutes by boiling. Jars should
be filled and sealed while still hot.

The recipes in this book were first
published in *Barbecue: delicious recipes
for outdoor cooking.*

contents

get sizzling

We associate barbecuing with being outdoors, and countries with warmer climates tend to be better equipped for this type of cooking. Now I am based in Australia, it has become very attractive indeed. The result is this book – a celebration of outdoor cooking on the barbecue.

The word 'barbecue' is derived from the Spanish word *barbacoa* and has several meanings: one is to cook over dry heat, such as coals; another is the equipment on which this is done; and a third is the meal itself – sometimes something as grand as a party. It seems to have originated in the Caribbean and Florida, then migrated across America's Deep South where barbecuing became a way of life. Barbecues as social gatherings can be traced back to when plantation owners held massive barbecues for friends, families and indeed their slaves.

For many of us, barbecuing has become one of our favourite methods of cooking – a simple, age-old way to cook that gives the food a unique flavour. There is something immensely pleasurable about cooking and eating outdoors. Firing up the barbecue is also the perfect excuse for a party. So, invite some friends and family round, get grilling and have fun.

little dishes

vegetable antipasto

Serving a large platter of grilled vegetables provides a lovely start to any barbecue – just select a combination of your favourites. A delicious way to serve them is on a bed of grilled polenta or accompanied by some fresh, crusty bread.

2 red peppers

4 baby fennel bulbs

1 large aubergine

1 red onion

2 large courgettes

1 recipe Herb, Lemon and Garlic Marinade (page 61)

a few fresh herb leaves, such as basil, dill, fennel, mint and parsley

extra virgin olive oil, to taste

lemon juice, to taste

sea salt and freshly ground black pepper

crusty bread or grilled polenta, to serve

serves 4

Cut the peppers into quarters and remove and discard the seeds. Trim the fennel, reserving the fronds, and cut the bulbs into 5 mm slices. Cut the aubergine into thick slices and cut in half again. Cut the onion into wedges and cut the courgettes into thick slices diagonally.

Put all the vegetables in a large bowl, add the marinade and toss gently until evenly coated. Let marinate in a cool place for at least 1 hour.

Preheat the barbecue, then cook the vegetables on the grill rack until they are all tender and lightly charred. Let cool, then peel the peppers.

Arrange the vegetables on a large platter, sprinkle with the herbs, reserved fennel fronds, olive oil and lemon juice, then season lightly with salt and pepper.

Serve at room temperature with slices of crusty bread or grilled polenta triangles.

9

Ripe figs filled with goats' cheese, then wrapped in prosciutto make a great first course. Prepare the salad in advance, but add the dressing at the last minute, otherwise it will become soggy.

fig, goats' cheese and prosciutto skewers with radicchio salad

Using a sharp knife, cut each fig lengthways into quarters without cutting all the way through. Cut the cheese into 8 equal pieces. Put a piece of cheese in the middle of each fig and close the figs. Wrap each fig with a slice of the ham and thread onto the skewers.

Preheat the barbecue. Cook the skewers over medium hot coals for 4–5 minutes, turning halfway through, until the ham is charred and the figs are sizzling.

To make the salad, tear the radicchio leaves into pieces and put in a bowl with the walnut pieces. Put the remaining ingredients in a separate bowl and whisk well. Pour the dressing over the leaves and toss until well coated. Serve with the fig skewers.

*Note To reduce balsamic vinegar, put 300 ml in a saucepan and bring to the boil. Boil gently until reduced by about two-thirds and it has reached the consistency of thick syrup. Let cool, then store in a clean jar or bottle.

8 large ripe figs

80 g goats' cheese

8 slices prosciutto

radicchio salad

1 head of radicchio, trimmed

a handful of walnut pieces, pan-toasted

4 tablespoons walnut oil

2 tablespoons extra virgin olive oil

1 tablespoon vincotto or Reduced Balsamic Vinegar*

sea salt and freshly ground black pepper

4 wooden skewers soaked in cold water for 30 minutes

serves 4

pepper 'n' spice chicken

Based on the classic Asian salt 'n' pepper squid, this delicious dish came about one day when I was playing around with a few spices and some chicken I had left over. It's now a family favourite. Serve with a squeeze of lime and some sweet chilli sauce.

Cut the chicken into 12 portions and put in a large, shallow dish. Sprinkle the rub and sesame oil over the chicken pieces and work in well. Let marinate in the refrigerator for 2 hours, then return to room temperature for 1 hour before cooking.

Preheat the barbecue. Cook the chicken over medium hot coals for 15–20 minutes, turning after 10 minutes, until the chicken is cooked through and the juices run clear when the thickest part of the meat is pierced with a skewer. Squeeze some lime juice over, let cool slightly, then serve with the sweet chilli sauce.

1 small chicken

1 recipe Fragrant Asian Rub (page 62)

2 tablespoons toasted sesame oil

1–2 limes, cut into wedges

Sweet Chilli Sauce (page 57), to serve

serves 4

20 uncooked prawns
250 g fillet steak
dipping sauces, to serve

prawn marinade
I teaspoon coriander seeds
½ teaspoon cumin seeds
I garlic clove, crushed
I teaspoon grated fresh ginger
2 kaffir lime leaves, shredded
I teaspoon ground turmeric
I tablespoon light soy sauce
4 tablespoons coconut milk
½ teaspoon salt

beef marinade
I garlic clove, crushed
2 stalks of lemongrass,
trimmed and finely chopped
I tablespoon grated
fresh ginger
4 coriander roots,
finely chopped
I red chilli, finely chopped
grated zest and juice of I lime
I tablespoon Thai fish sauce
I tablespoon dark soy sauce
I½ tablespoons sugar
I tablespoon sesame oil
freshly ground black pepper

*40 wooden skewers soaked in
cold water for 30 minutes*

serves 4

prawn and beef satays

**Satays are found all over South-east Asia. They
are very easy to make and taste simply wonderful.**

Shell and devein the prawns. Wash them under cold running water
and pat dry with kitchen paper. Put them in a shallow dish.

To make the prawn marinade, put the coriander and cumin seeds
in a dry frying pan and toast over medium heat until golden and
aromatic. Remove, let cool slightly, then transfer to a spice grinder
(or a clean coffee grinder). Add the garlic, ginger and lime leaves to
the grinder and grind to a coarse paste. Alternatively, use a mortar
and pestle to make the paste.

Transfer the paste to a bowl, add the turmeric, soy sauce, coconut
milk and salt and mix well. Pour the marinade over the prawns and
let marinate in the refrigerator for I hour.

To make the beef satays, cut the fillet steak across the grain into thin
strips. Mix all the ingredients for the beef marinade in a shallow dish,
add the beef strips and let marinate in the refrigerator for I hour.

Preheat the barbecue. To assemble the beef satays, thread the beef
strips onto the soaked skewers, zig-zagging back and forth as you
go. To assemble the prawn satays, thread the prawns lengthways
onto the skewers.

Cook both kinds of satays over hot coals for 2 minutes each side,
brushing the beef marinade over the beef satays halfway through.
Serve hot with your choice of dipping sauces.

salads & sides

This satisfying summer salad with a delicious hint of fresh mint makes a superb accompaniment to any barbecued meat or fish.

courgette, feta and mint salad

1 tablespoon sesame seeds

6 large courgettes

3 tablespoons extra virgin olive oil

150 g feta cheese, crumbled

a handful of fresh mint leaves

dressing

4 tablespoons extra virgin olive oil

1 tablespoon lemon juice

1 small garlic clove, crushed

sea salt and freshly ground black pepper

serves 4

Put the sesame seeds in a dry frying pan and toast over medium heat until golden and aromatic. Remove from the heat, let cool and set aside until required.

Preheat the barbecue. Cut the courgettes diagonally into thick slices, toss with the olive oil and season with salt and pepper. Cook over hot coals for 2–3 minutes on each side until charred and tender. Remove and let cool.

Put all the dressing ingredients in a screw-top jar and shake well. Add salt and pepper to taste.

Put the courgettes, feta and mint in a large bowl, add the dressing and toss well until evenly coated. Sprinkle with the toasted sesame seeds and serve at once.

salad of roasted peppers and asparagus

Vegetables taste wonderful when cooked on the barbecue – it brings out their natural sweetness. Look out for the long, thin red peppers (ramiro or romano) when available – they are particularly good grilled. This salad serves four as a main course or six as a starter.

Put the sliced onion in a sieve, sprinkle with salt and let drain over a bowl for 30 minutes. Rinse well under cold running water and pat dry with kitchen paper.

Preheat the barbecue, then cook the whole peppers over hot coals for 15 minutes, turning frequently until charred all over. Transfer to a plastic bag, seal and let soften until cool. Peel off the skin and discard the seeds, then cut the flesh into thick strips.

Brush the asparagus with olive oil and cook over hot coals for 3–4 minutes, turning frequently, until charred and tender.

Put the mangetout in a large saucepan of lightly salted boiling water and boil for 1–2 minutes. Drain and refresh under cold running water.

Put all the dressing ingredients in a bowl and whisk well. Put the onion, peppers, asparagus and mangetout in a large bowl and toss gently. Add the salad leaves, herbs and hazelnuts. Pour over the dressing and toss until well coated. Serve immediately.

½ red onion, sliced

6 sweet red peppers

500 g asparagus spears, trimmed

extra virgin olive oil, for brushing

250 g mangetout

75 g mixed salad leaves

a handful of fresh flat leaf parsley and dill leaves

50 g hazelnuts, toasted and coarsely chopped

hazelnut oil dressing

4 tablespoons hazelnut oil

2 tablespoons extra virgin olive oil

1 tablespoon sherry vinegar

1 teaspoon caster sugar

sea salt and freshly ground black pepper

serves 4–6

tomato and grilled bread salad

This is just one of those dishes I make over and over again, particularly in the summer when tomatoes are so good. For the best flavour, use vine-ripened tomatoes. If sourdough bread is unavailable, use ciabatta instead.

Preheat the barbecue, then grill the bread slices over hot coals for 1 minute on each side or until toasted and charred. Remove from the heat, rub all over with the garlic cloves, then sprinkle with 2 tablespoons of the oil. Let cool, then cut into cubes.

Put the grilled bread cubes in a large bowl and add the tomatoes and olives. Put the vinegar and remaining olive oil in a separate bowl and mix well, then pour over the salad. Season with salt and pepper and stir well.

Set aside to infuse for 30 minutes, then stir in the basil leaves and serve.

4 slices sourdough bread

2 garlic cloves, peeled but left whole

8 tablespoons extra virgin olive oil

650 g vine-ripened tomatoes, coarsely chopped

50 g pitted black olives

1 tablespoon aged balsamic vinegar

a handful of fresh basil leaves, torn

sea salt and freshly ground black pepper

serves 4–6

In this version of the famous recipe, corn-on-the-cob steams inside the husks first, then has a short blast over the hot coals to brown and flavour the kernels. Delicious served with plenty of crusty bread to mop up the juices.

grilled **corn-on-the-cob**

4 corn cobs, unhusked

125 g butter

1 garlic clove, crushed

2 teaspoons chopped fresh thyme

grated zest of 1 unwaxed lemon

sea salt and freshly ground black pepper

crusty bread, to serve

serves 4

Carefully peel back the husks from the corn, but leave them attached at the stalk. Remove and discard the cornsilk. Fold the husks back in position and tie in place with string. Put the corn in a large bowl of cold water, let soak for 30 minutes, then drain and pat dry with kitchen paper.

Preheat the barbecue, then cook the corn over medium hot coals for 15 minutes, turning regularly until the outer husks are evenly charred. Remove from the heat, let cool slightly, then remove the husks. Return to the grill rack and cook for a further 8–10 minutes, turning frequently until the kernels are lightly charred.

Meanwhile, put the butter, garlic, thyme, lemon zest, salt and pepper in a small saucepan and heat gently until the butter has melted. Sprinkle the butter mixture over the cooked corn cobs and serve hot with crusty bread.

garlic bread skewers

This is a fun version of garlic bread, and the slightly smoky flavour you get from the coals is delicious. You can also add cubes of cheese such as mozzarella or fontina to the skewers.

1 baguette

150 ml extra virgin olive oil

2 garlic cloves, crushed

2 tablespoons chopped fresh flat leaf parsley

sea salt and freshly ground black pepper

6–8 wooden skewers soaked in cold water for 30 minutes

serves 6–8

Cut the bread into 2 cm thick slices, then cut the slices crossways to make half moons.

Put the olive oil, garlic, parsley, salt and pepper in a large bowl, add the bread and toss until well coated.

Preheat the barbecue. Thread the garlic bread onto skewers and cook over medium hot coals for 2–3 minutes on each side until evenly toasted.

Variation

Cut 250 g mozzarella cheese into about 24 pieces. Thread a piece of bread onto a skewer, then a cube of cheese and continue to alternate the cheese and bread. Cook as in the main recipe.

Hot from the grill, this aromatic herb bread is delicious used to mop up any wonderful meat juices or eaten on its own with olive oil for dipping.

grilled **rosemary flatbread**

250 g strong white flour, plus extra for dusting

1½ teaspoons fast-acting yeast

1 teaspoon salt

1 tablespoon chopped fresh rosemary

120 ml hot water

2 tablespoons extra virgin olive oil, plus extra for brushing

serves 4

Sift the flour into the bowl of an electric mixer and stir in the yeast, salt and rosemary. Add the hot water and olive oil and knead with the dough hook at high speed for about 8 minutes or until the dough is smooth and elastic. Alternatively, sift the flour into a large bowl and stir in the yeast, salt and rosemary. Make a well in the centre, then add the hot water and olive oil and mix to form a soft dough. Turn out onto a lightly floured work surface and knead until the dough is smooth and elastic.

Shape the dough into a ball, then put it in an oiled bowl. Cover with a tea towel and let rise in a warm place for 45–60 minutes, or until doubled in size.

Punch down the dough and divide into quarters. Roll each piece out on a lightly floured work surface to make a 15 cm long oval.

Preheat the barbecue. Brush the bread with a little olive oil and cook for 5 minutes over low heat. Brush the top with the remaining olive oil, flip and cook for a further 4–5 minutes until the bread is cooked through. Serve hot.

fish & seafood

red snapper with parsley salad

Even if the snapper has already been scaled by the fishmonger, go over it again to remove any stray scales – they are huge! You could use a fish grilling basket to cook this fish, if you have one.

4 red snapper, cleaned and well scaled, about 350 g each

1 recipe Herb, Lemon and Garlic Marinade (page 61)

parsley salad

50 g raisins

2 tablespoons verjuice* or white grape juice

leaves from a large bunch of fresh flat leaf parsley

25 g pine nuts, toasted

50 g feta cheese, crumbled

3 tablespoons extra virgin olive oil

2 teaspoons balsamic vinegar

sea salt and freshly ground black pepper

serves 4

Using a sharp knife, cut several slashes into each side of the fish. Put them in a shallow ceramic dish and pour over the marinade. Let marinate in the refrigerator for 4 hours, then return to room temperature for 1 hour before cooking.

Just before cooking the fish, make the salad. Put the raisins in a bowl, add the verjuice and let soak for 15 minutes. Drain and set the liquid aside. Put the parsley, pine nuts, soaked raisins and feta in a bowl. Put the olive oil, vinegar and reserved raisin liquid in a separate bowl and mix well. Pour over the salad and toss until well coated. Season with salt and pepper.

Preheat the barbecue, then cook the fish over hot coals for 4–5 minutes on each side. Let rest briefly before serving with the parsley salad.

*Note Verjuice, which is used in the salad dressing, is produced from the juice of unripe grapes. It is available from Italian delicatessens. If you can't find it, use white grape juice instead.

hot-smoked **creole salmon**

4 salmon fillets,
skinned, about
200 g each

I recipe Creole Rub
(page 62)

a large handful of
wood chips, such as
hickory, soaked in cold
water for I hour,
drained

I recipe Mango and
Sesame Salsa
(page 58)

serves 4

Wash the salmon under cold running water and pat dry with kitchen paper. Using a pair of tweezers, pull out any bones, then put the fish in a dish and work the Creole rub all over it. Let marinate in the refrigerator for at least I hour.

Preheat the barbecue. When the coals are hot, rake them into two piles at either side of the grill and put a foil drip tray in the middle. Tip half the soaked wood chips onto each pile of coals.

As soon as the wood chips start to smoke, put the salmon fillets on the centre of the grill. Cover with the lid, leaving any air vents open. Cook for 15–20 minutes, or until the salmon is cooked through. To test the fish, press the salmon with your finger, the flesh should feel firm and start to open into flakes. Serve hot or cold with the mango and sesame salsa.

Smoking food on the barbecue is simply magical – the flavours are truly wonderful. You will need a barbecue with a lid for this recipe. If you have a gas barbecue follow the manufacturer's instructions for indirect grill-smoking.

salt-crusted prawns
with tomato, avocado and olive salad

Coating the prawns with sea salt protects the flesh during cooking so that when you shell them, the meat inside is sweet and moist.

To prepare the salad, put the tomatoes and avocado on a plate with the olives and mint. Put the olive oil and vinegar in a jug and stir well, then pour over the salad. Sprinkle over the Parmesan shavings and add salt and pepper to taste.

To prepare the prawns, use kitchen scissors to cut down the back of each prawn to reveal the intestinal vein. Pull it out and discard. Wash the prawns under cold running water, pat dry with kitchen paper and put in a bowl. Add the olive oil and toss well. Put the salt on a plate and use to coat the prawns.

Preheat the barbecue, then cook the prawns over hot coals for 2–3 minutes on each side until cooked through. Let cool slightly, peel off the shells and serve with the tomato, avocado and olive salad, lemon wedges and salad leaves.

20 large uncooked prawns

1 tablespoon extra virgin olive oil

3 tablespoons salt

tomato, avocado and olive salad

4–6 large ripe tomatoes, sliced

1 large ripe avocado, halved, stoned and sliced

50 g pitted black olives

a handful of fresh mint leaves

4 tablespoons extra virgin olive oil

1 tablespoon Reduced Balsamic Vinegar (see page 10)

shavings of fresh Parmesan cheese

sea salt and freshly ground black pepper

to serve

lemon wedges

salad leaves

serves 4

dukkah-crusted tuna
with preserved lemon salsa

Dukkah is a Middle Eastern dish comprising mixed nuts and spices, which are ground to a coarse powder and served as a dip for warm bread. Here, it is used as a coating for grilled tuna. Preserved lemons are available from good delicatessens and Middle Eastern food stores.

To make the salsa, chop the preserved lemon and tomatoes finely and put in a bowl. Stir in the spring onions, parsley, olive oil and sugar and set aside until ready to serve.

Wash the tuna steaks under cold running water and pat dry with kitchen paper.

Put the sesame seeds in a dry frying pan and toast over medium heat until golden and aromatic. Remove and let cool. Repeat with the coriander seeds, cumin seeds and almonds. Transfer all the seeds and nuts to a spice grinder (or a clean coffee grinder) and grind roughly. Alternatively, use a mortar and pestle. Add the salt and a little pepper.

Preheat the barbecue. Brush the tuna steaks with olive oil and coat with the dukkah mixture. Cook over hot coals for 1 minute on each side, top with the salsa and serve.

4 tuna steaks, about 200 g each

3 tablespoons sesame seeds

2 tablespoons coriander seeds

½ tablespoon cumin seeds

25 g blanched almonds, chopped

½ teaspoon salt

freshly ground black pepper

olive oil, for brushing

preserved lemon salsa

25 g preserved lemon

25 g semi-dried tomatoes

2 spring onions, very finely chopped

1 tablespoon coarsely chopped fresh flat leaf parsley

3 tablespoons extra virgin olive oil

¼ teaspoon caster sugar

serves 4

meat & poultry

This spice dip, called zahtar, is served with pita bread. It is sold ready-made from Middle Eastern stores, but it is very easy to make your own.

chicken skewers
with thyme and sesame dip

3 tablespoons Zahtar Spice Mix (see below)

3 tablespoons extra virgin olive oil

750 g boneless chicken breast fillets

zahtar spice mix

3 tablespoons sesame seeds

30 g fresh thyme leaves

½ teaspoon salt

to serve

chilli oil

1–2 lemons, cut into wedges

mixed salad leaves

8 wooden skewers soaked in cold water for 30 minutes

serves 4

To make the zahtar spice mix, put the sesame seeds in a dry frying pan and toast over medium heat until golden and aromatic. Remove, let cool, then transfer to a spice grinder (or a clean coffee grinder). Add the thyme leaves and salt, then blend to a coarse powder. Alternatively, use a mortar and pestle. You will need 3 tablespoons of the mix for this recipe. Put the remainder in an airtight container and keep in a cool place for future use.

Put the 3 tablespoons of zahtar spice mix and the olive oil in a shallow dish and mix well. Cut the chicken into bite-sized pieces, add to the zahtar oil and toss well until coated. Let marinate in the refrigerator for at least 2 hours.

Preheat the barbecue, then thread the chicken pieces onto the soaked wooden skewers and cook over hot coals for 2–3 minutes on each side. Remove from the heat, let rest briefly, then sprinkle with chilli oil and lemon juice and serve hot with salad leaves.

tea-smoked asian spiced duck breast

The tea-smoke mixture adds a lovely spicy aroma to the duck. I like to cook the duck with the skin on, but this can be removed after cooking, if preferred. You will need a barbecue with a lid. If you have a gas barbecue follow the manufacturer's instructions for indirect grill-smoking.

Using a sharp knife, cut several slashes in the duck skin, then put the duck in a shallow dish. Add the Thai spice marinade, cover and let marinate in the refrigerator overnight. Remove from the refrigerator 1 hour before cooking.

Preheat the barbecue. When the coals are hot, rake them into two piles at either side of the grill and put a foil drip tray in the middle.

Put all the ingredients for the tea-smoke mixture in a bowl and mix well. Transfer to a sheet of foil, fold the edges over and around the smoke mixture, seal well, then pierce the foil in about 10 places.

Put the foil parcel directly on top of the hot coals, cover with the barbecue lid and wait until smoke appears. Remove the duck from the marinade and put onto the grill rack over the drip tray. Cover with the lid and cook for 15 minutes until the duck is cooked through. Discard the marinade.

Let the duck rest briefly, then serve with the mango and sesame salsa and salad leaves.

4 duck breast fillets, about 200 g each

1 recipe Thai Spice Marinade (page 61)

tea-smoke mixture

8 tablespoons soft brown sugar

8 tablespoons long grain rice

8 tablespoons tea leaves

2 cinnamon sticks, bruised

1 star anise

to serve

Mango and Sesame Salsa (page 58)

Asian salad leaves

serves 4

This hot dog recipe calls for good-quality pork sausages rather than the more typical frankfurters usually associated with hot dogs. I think this version tastes great, especially with the caramelized onions and wholegrain mustard.

top dogs

Put the onion wedges in a bowl, add the olive oil, sage and a little salt and pepper and mix well. Preheat the flat plate on a gas barbecue and cook the onions for 15–20 minutes, stirring occasionally until golden and tender. If you have a charcoal barbecue, cook the onions in a frying pan on top of the stove or on the barbecue. Keep the onions hot.

Meanwhile, cook the sausages over hot coals for 10–12 minutes, turning frequently until charred and cooked through. Transfer to a plate and let rest briefly.

Cut the hot dog rolls almost in half, then put onto the grill rack and toast for a few minutes. Remove from the heat and spread with mustard. Fill with the tomatoes, sausages and onions. Add a little barbecue sauce, if using, and serve hot.

2 onions, cut into thin wedges

2–3 tablespoons extra virgin olive oil

1 tablespoon chopped fresh sage

4 good-quality pork sausages, pricked

4 hot dog rolls

4 tablespoons wholegrain mustard

2 ripe tomatoes, sliced

sea salt and freshly ground black pepper

Barbecue Sauce (page 57), to serve (optional)

serves 4

smoky barbecue ribs

These grilled ribs are spicy, smoky, sticky, tender and lip-smackingly good. They may take a little time to prepare because of soaking and marinating, but they are simple to cook and definitely well worth the effort.

Wash the ribs under cold running water and pat dry with kitchen paper. Put the ribs in a large dish, add the vinegar and let soak for 4 hours or overnight. Rinse the ribs well and pat dry with kitchen paper.

Put the sugar, salt, paprika, pepper, onion powder, garlic powder and cayenne pepper in a bowl and mix well. Rub the mixture all over the ribs and let marinate in the refrigerator for 2 hours.

To make the creamy coleslaw, put the cabbage, carrots and onion in a colander and sprinkle with the salt, sugar and vinegar. Stir well and let drain over a bowl for 30 minutes.

Squeeze out excess liquid from the vegetables, then put them in a large bowl. Put the mayonnaise, cream and mustard in a separate bowl and mix well, then stir into the cabbage mixture. Season to taste with salt and pepper.

Preheat the barbecue, then cook the ribs over low heat for 20 minutes on each side. Brush all over with the barbecue sauce and cook for a further 15 minutes on each side until the ribs are lightly charred, tender and sticky. Remove and let cool briefly before serving with the creamy coleslaw.

2 racks pork spare ribs, about 650 g each

300 ml white wine vinegar

2 tablespoons soft brown sugar

1 tablespoon salt

1 tablespoon sweet paprika

2 teaspoons crushed black pepper

2 teaspoons onion powder

1 teaspoon garlic powder

¼ teaspoon cayenne pepper

150 ml Barbecue Sauce (page 57)

creamy coleslaw

250 g white cabbage, thinly sliced

175 g carrots, grated

½ white onion, thinly sliced

1 teaspoon salt

2 teaspoons caster sugar

1 tablespoon white wine vinegar

50 g mayonnaise

2 tablespoons double cream

1 tablespoon wholegrain mustard

sea salt and freshly ground black pepper

serves 4

vietnamese pork balls

1 stalk of lemongrass

500 g minced pork

125 g pork belly, minced

25 g breadcrumbs

6 kaffir lime leaves, very finely sliced

2 garlic cloves, crushed

2 cm fresh ginger, grated

1 fresh red chilli, deseeded and chopped

2 tablespoons Thai fish sauce (*nam pla*)

to serve

lettuce leaves

a handful of fresh herb leaves, such as mint, coriander and Thai basil

Sweet Chilli Sauce (page 57)

4 wooden skewers soaked in cold water for 30 minutes

serves 4

Like many Vietnamese dishes, these delicious pork balls are served wrapped in a lettuce leaf with plenty of fresh herbs and sweet chilli sauce.

Using a sharp knife, trim the lemongrass stalk to about 15 cm in length, then remove and discard the tough outer leaves. Chop the inner stalk very finely.

Put the minced pork, pork belly and breadcrumbs in a bowl, then add the lemongrass, lime leaves, garlic, ginger, chilli and fish sauce and mix well. Let marinate in the refrigerator for at least 1 hour.

Preheat the barbecue, then brush the grill rack with oil. Using your hands, shape the pork mixture into 20 small balls and carefully thread 5 onto each of the soaked wooden skewers. Cook the skewers over hot coals for 5–6 minutes, turning halfway through, until cooked.

Serve the pork balls wrapped in the lettuce leaves and herbs with the sweet chilli sauce on the side for dipping.

Choosing the right cut of meat for barbecue cooking is the first step to producing the perfect steak. There are several cuts you can use, such as fillet, T-bone or sirloin, but my own favourite is rib eye steak. As the name suggests, it is the 'eye' of the rib roast and is marbled with fat, giving a moist result. It has a good flavour and is not too huge.

rib eye steak with anchovy butter

125 g butter, softened

8 anchovy fillets in oil, drained and chopped coarsely

2 tablespoons chopped fresh flat leaf parsley

4 rib eye steaks, about 250 g each

sea salt and freshly ground black pepper

serves 4

Put the butter, anchovies, parsley and a little pepper in a bowl and beat well. Transfer to a sheet of foil and roll up into a log shape. Chill until required.

Preheat the barbecue and brush the grill rack with oil. Season the steaks with salt and pepper and cook over hot coals for 3 minutes on each side for rare, 4–5 minutes for medium and about 5–6 minutes for well done.

Transfer the steaks to a warmed serving plate and put 2 slices of anchovy butter on each one. Let rest for about 5 minutes before serving, in order to set the juices.

butterflied lamb
with white bean salad

1.5–2 kg leg of lamb, butterflied

I recipe Herb, Lemon and Garlic Marinade (page 61)

I recipe Salsa Verde (page 59), to serve

white bean salad

I large red onion, finely chopped

3 cans haricot beans, about 400 g each, drained

2 garlic cloves, chopped

3 tomatoes, deseeded and chopped

75 ml extra virgin olive oil

1½ tablespoons red wine vinegar

2 tablespoons chopped fresh flat leaf parsley

sea salt and freshly ground black pepper

serves 8

This is probably the best way to cook lamb on the barbecue — the bone is removed and the meat opened out flat so it can cook quickly and evenly over the coals. If you don't fancy boning the lamb yourself, ask your butcher to do it for you.

To make the white bean salad, put the onion in a colander, sprinkle with salt and let drain over a bowl for 30 minutes. Wash the onion under cold running water and dry well. Transfer to a bowl, then add the beans, garlic, tomatoes, olive oil, vinegar, parsley and salt and pepper to taste.

Put the lamb in a shallow dish, pour over the marinade, cover and let marinate in the refrigerator overnight. Remove from the refrigerator 1 hour before cooking.

Preheat the barbecue. Drain the lamb and discard the marinade. Cook over medium hot coals for 12–15 minutes on each side until charred on the outside but still pink in the middle (cook for a little longer if you prefer the meat less rare). Let the lamb rest for 10 minutes.

Cut the lamb into medium slices and serve with the white bean salad and salsa verde.

sweet things

grilled fruit parcels

Wrapping fruits in foil is a great way to cook them on the barbecue – all the juices are contained in the parcel while the fruit softens.

4 peaches or nectarines, halved, stoned and sliced

200 g blueberries

125 g raspberries

juice of 1 orange

1 teaspoon ground cinnamon

2 tablespoons caster sugar

200 g thick yoghurt

1 tablespoon clear honey

1 tablespoon rosewater

1 tablespoon chopped pistachio nuts

serves 4

Put the fruit in a large bowl, add the orange juice, cinnamon and sugar and mix well. Divide the fruit mixture between 4 sheets of foil. Fold the foil over the fruit and seal the edges to make parcels.

Put the yoghurt, honey and rosewater in a separate bowl and mix well. Set aside until required.

Preheat the barbecue, then cook the parcels over medium hot coals for 5–6 minutes. Remove the parcels from the heat, open carefully and transfer to 4 serving bowls. Serve with the yoghurt and a sprinkling of pistachio nuts.

This dish works well with stone fruits too, such as plums, peaches or nectarines.

grilled figs
with almond mascarpone cream

To make the almond mascarpone cream, put the mascarpone cheese, vanilla essence, almonds, Marsala wine and honey in a bowl and beat well. Set aside in the refrigerator until required.

Put the sugar and ground cardamom in a separate bowl and mix well, then carefully dip the cut surfaces of the figs into the mixture.

Preheat the barbecue, then cook the figs over medium hot coals for 1–2 minutes on each side until charred and softened.

Transfer the grilled figs to 4 serving bowls and serve with the almond mascarpone cream.

150 g mascarpone cheese

½ teaspoon vanilla essence

1 tablespoon toasted ground almonds

1 tablespoon Marsala wine

1 tablespoon clear honey

1 tablespoon caster sugar

1 teaspoon ground cardamom

8–10 figs, halved

serves 4

s'mores

This is one for the kids. S'mores are an American campfire classic where graham crackers, barbecued marshmallows and chocolate squares are sandwiched together to make a delicious, gooey taste sensation.
I prefer to use a sweet biscuit, such as langue du chat or almond thins instead of graham crackers, but any will do.

Put half the biscuits on a plate and top each one with a square of chocolate.

Preheat the barbecue. Thread 2 marshmallows onto each skewer and cook over hot coals for about 2 minutes, turning constantly until the marshmallows are melted and blackened. Remove from the heat and let cool slightly.

Put the marshmallows on the chocolate squares and sandwich together with the remaining biscuits. Gently ease out the skewers and serve the s'mores as soon as the chocolate melts.

16 biscuits

8 pieces of plain chocolate

16 marshmallows

8 metal skewers

serves 4

basics

barbecue sauce

200 ml tomato passata

100 ml maple syrup

50 ml dark treacle

50 ml tomato ketchup

50 ml white wine vinegar

3 tablespoons Worcestershire sauce

1 tablespoon Dijon mustard

1 teaspoon garlic powder

¼ teaspoon hot paprika

sea salt and freshly ground black pepper

makes about 400 ml

Put all the ingredients in a small saucepan, bring to the boil and simmer gently for 10–15 minutes until reduced slightly and thickened. Season to taste with salt and pepper and let cool.

Pour into an airtight container and store in the refrigerator for up to 2 weeks.

sweet chilli sauce

6 large red chillies, deseeded and chopped

4 garlic cloves, chopped

1 teaspoon grated fresh ginger

1 teaspoon salt

100 ml rice wine vinegar

100 ml sugar

makes about 200 ml

Put the chillies, garlic, ginger and salt in a food processor and blend to a coarse paste. Transfer to a saucepan, add the vinegar and sugar, bring to the boil and simmer gently, part-covered, for 5 minutes until the mixture becomes a thin syrup. Remove from the heat and let cool.

Pour into an airtight container and store in the refrigerator for up to 2 weeks.

asian barbecue sauce

100 ml tomato passata

50 ml hoisin sauce

1 teaspoon hot chilli sauce

2 garlic cloves, crushed

2 tablespoons sweet soy sauce

1 tablespoon rice wine vinegar

1 teaspoon ground coriander

½ teaspoon ground cinnamon

¼ teaspoon Chinese five-spice powder

makes about 350 ml

Put all the ingredients in a small saucepan, add 100 ml water, bring to the boil and simmer gently for 10 minutes. Remove from the heat and let cool.

Pour into an airtight container and store in the refrigerator for up to 2 weeks.

Note The recipe for Reduced Balsamic Vinegar (far right) is given on page 10.

smoky tomato salsa

4 ripe plum tomatoes

2 large fresh red chillies

4 whole garlic cloves, peeled

1 red onion, quartered

4 tablespoons extra virgin olive oil

1 tablespoon lemon juice

2 tablespoons chopped fresh coriander

sea salt and freshly ground black pepper

2 wooden skewers, soaked in cold water for 30 minutes

makes about 500 ml

Using tongs, hold the tomatoes over the flames of the barbecue for about 1 minute, turning frequently, until the skin is charred all over. Let cool, peel, cut in half and remove and discard the seeds, then chop the flesh. Repeat with the chillies.

Thread the garlic cloves and onion wedges onto separate skewers. Cook the garlic over hot coals for 5–6 minutes and the onion for 10–12 minutes, turning frequently, until they are charred and softened. Let cool, remove from the skewers and cut into cubes.

Put the tomato, chillies, garlic and onion in a bowl and stir in the oil, lemon juice and coriander. Season to taste with salt and pepper and use as required. Alternatively, spoon the salsa into sterilized jars and seal tightly. Store in the refrigerator until you are ready to use.

mango and sesame salsa

1 large ripe mango

4 spring onions, trimmed and finely chopped

1 small red chilli, deseeded and chopped

1 garlic clove, crushed

1 tablespoon light soy sauce

1 tablespoon lime juice

1 teaspoon sesame oil

½ tablespoon caster sugar

1 tablespoon chopped fresh coriander

sea salt and freshly ground black pepper

makes about 200 ml

Peel the mango and cut the flesh away from the pit. Cut the flesh into cubes and mix with all the remaining ingredients and season to taste.

Set aside for 30 minutes for the flavours to infuse before serving.

salsa verde

a bunch of parsley
(about 25 g)

a small bunch of mixed fresh herbs
such as basil, chives and mint

1 garlic clove, chopped

1 tablespoon pitted green olives

1 tablespoon capers, drained
and rinsed

2 anchovy fillets, rinsed
and chopped

1 teaspoon Dijon mustard

2 teaspoons white wine vinegar

150 ml extra virgin olive oil

sea salt and freshly ground
black pepper

---

makes about 200 ml

Put all the ingredients except the
oil in a food processor and blend
to a smooth paste. Gradually
pour in the oil to form a sauce,
then taste and adjust the
seasoning. The salsa may be
stored in the refrigerator for
up to 3 days.

thai spice marinade

2 stalks of lemongrass

6 kaffir lime leaves

2 garlic cloves, coarsely chopped

2 cm fresh ginger, coarsely chopped

4 coriander roots, washed and dried

2 small fresh red chillies, deseeded and coarsely chopped

200 ml extra virgin olive oil

2 tablespoons sesame oil

2 tablespoons Thai fish sauce (*nam pla*)

---

makes about 300 ml

Using a sharp knife, trim the lemongrass stalks to 15 cm, then remove and discard the tough outer layers. Chop the inner stalks coarsely.

Put the lemongrass stalks, lime leaves, garlic, ginger, coriander roots and chillies in a mortar and pound with a pestle to release the aromas.

Transfer the mixture to a bowl, add the oils and fish sauce and set aside to infuse until you are ready to marinate.

minted yoghurt marinade

2 teaspoons coriander seeds

1 teaspoon cumin seeds

250 ml thick yoghurt

juice of ½ lemon

1 tablespoon extra virgin olive oil

2 garlic cloves, crushed

1 teaspoon grated fresh ginger

½ teaspoon salt

2 tablespoons chopped fresh mint

¼ teaspoon chilli powder

---

makes about 275 ml

Put the coriander and cumin seeds in a dry frying pan and toast over medium heat until golden and aromatic. Remove from the heat and let cool. Transfer to a spice grinder (or a clean coffee grinder) and crush to a coarse powder. Alternatively, use a mortar and pestle.

Put the spices in a bowl, add the yoghurt, lemon juice, olive oil, garlic, ginger, salt, mint and chilli powder and mix well. Set aside to infuse until you are ready to marinate.

herb, lemon and garlic marinade

2 sprigs of rosemary

2 sprigs of thyme

4 bay leaves

2 large garlic cloves, coarsely chopped

pared zest of 1 unwaxed lemon

1 teaspoon black peppercorns, coarsely crushed

200 ml extra virgin olive oil

---

makes about 300 ml

Strip the rosemary and thyme leaves from the stalks and put in a mortar. Add the bay leaves, garlic and lemon zest and pound with a pestle to release the aromas.

Put the mixture in a bowl and add the peppercorns and olive oil. Set aside to infuse until you are ready to marinate.

creole rub

½ small onion, finely chopped
I garlic clove, finely chopped
I tablespoon chopped fresh thyme
I tablespoon paprika
I teaspoon ground cumin
I teaspoon table salt
¼ teaspoon cayenne pepper
I tablespoon brown sugar
a little freshly ground black pepper

makes about 6 tablespoons

Put all the ingredients in a small bowl, mix well and set aside to infuse until you are ready to use.

moroccan rub

I tablespoon coriander seeds
I teaspoon cumin seeds
2 cinnamon sticks
I teaspoon whole allspice berries
6 cloves
a pinch of saffron threads
I teaspoon ground turmeric
2 teaspoons dried onion flakes
I teaspoon salt
½ teaspoon paprika

makes about 6 tablespoons

Put the whole spices and saffron threads in a dry frying pan and toast over medium heat for about 1–2 minutes or until golden and aromatic. Remove from the heat and let cool. Transfer to a spice grinder (or a clean coffee grinder) and crush to a coarse powder. Alternatively, use a mortar and pestle.

Put the spices in a bowl, add the remaining ingredients and mix well. Set aside to infuse until you are ready to use.

fragrant asian rub

4 whole star anise
2 teaspoons Szechuan peppercorns
I teaspoon fennel seeds
2 small pieces of cassia bark
or I cinnamon stick, broken
6 cloves
2 garlic cloves, finely chopped
grated zest of 2 unwaxed limes
I teaspoon salt

makes about 6 tablespoons

Put the whole spices in a dry frying pan and toast over medium heat for 1–2 minutes or until golden and aromatic. Remove from the heat and let cool. Transfer to a spice grinder (or a clean coffee grinder) and crush to a coarse powder. Alternatively, use a mortar and pestle.

Put the spices in a bowl, add the garlic, lime zest and salt and mix well. Set aside to infuse until you are ready to use.

index